A Child's History of Britain

Life in
Medieval Britain

Anita Ganeri

Raintree

Raintree is an imprint of Capstone Global Library Limited, a company incorporated in England and Wales having its registered office at 7 Pilgrim Street, London, EC4V 6LB – Registered company number: 6695582

www.raintreepublishers.co.uk
myorders@raintreepublishers.co.uk

Edited by Nick Hunter and Penny West
Designed by Joanna Malivoire
Original illustration © Capstone Global Library Ltd 2014
Illustrated by: Laszlo Veres (pp.26-7), Beehive Illustration
Picture research by Mica Brancic
Originated by Capstone Global Library Ltd
Production by Helen McCreath
Printed and bound in China

ISBN 978 1 406 27050 1
18 17 16 15 14
10 9 8 7 6 5 4 3 2 1

British Library Cataloguing in Publication Data
A full catalogue record for this book is available from the British Library.

Acknowledgements

We would like to thank the following for permission to reproduce photographs: © Crown Copyright (2013) Visit Wales p. 27 top (CADW); Alamy pp. 11 (© North Wind Picture Archives), 12 (© Louise Heusinkveld), 13 (© Walker Art Library), 18 (© Justin Kase z05z), 20 (© Lebrecht Music and Arts Photo Library), 21 (© Purple Marbles York 1), 27 bottom (© Nearby); Corbis pp. 6 (© The Print Collector), 7 (© Stapleton Collection), 15 (© Heritage Images), 23 (© Bettmann), 24 (© Stapleton Collection); Getty Images pp. 5 (Universal Images Group/Universal History Archive), 10 (Hulton Archive), 14 (Archive Photos/Buyenlarge), 19 (Hulton Archive), 22 (Hulton Archive), 25 (The Bridgeman Art Library/Private Collection); Robert Harding World Imagery p. 17 (© Roy Rainford); Shutterstock pp. 9 (© Gail Johnson), 16 (© Pawel Kowalczyk); SuperStock p. 8 (The Francis Frith Collection).
Cover photograph of a medieval knight helping two peasant children over a river reproduced with permission of The Bridgeman Art Library (© Lady Lever Art Gallery, National Museums Liverpool).

We would like to thank Heather Montgomery for her invaluable help in the preparation of this book.

Disclaimer

Contents

Some words are shown in bold, **like this**. You can find out what they mean by looking in the glossary.

Medieval Britain

The medieval period in Britain covered over 400 years from 1066 to 1485. It was a time of many wars. It was also a time when many great castles and cathedrals were built.

A TIME OF WARS

1066	Battle of Hastings
1282	Edward I conquers Wales
1296	Edward I invades Scotland
1314	Battle of Bannockburn – the Scots defeat the English
1337–1453	Hundred Years' War with France
1455–1485	Wars of the Roses

William the Conqueror

In 1066, Edward, King of England died. He had no children to take over as king. Three people claimed his throne: Harold, Earl of Wessex, a powerful English nobleman; William, Duke of Normandy; and Harald Hardrada, a Viking king. Harold killed Harald Hardrada. Then, at the Battle of Hastings in 1066, William's troops defeated Harold's army. Harold died after being shot in the eye with an arrow.

THE BAYEUX TAPESTRY

The Bayeux Tapestry tells the story of the Battle of Hastings in pictures, like a cartoon strip. It is 70 metres (230 feet) long.

The Bayeux Tapestry was probably sewn in Canterbury in the 11th century.

The victory at the Battle of Hastings earned William the title "Conqueror". He was crowned king of England on Christmas Day 1066.

Who was in charge?

The king and his nobles were the most powerful people in medieval times. The **bishops** and **abbots** were also very important. They were in charge of the cathedrals and **monasteries**. The king, his nobles, and the church owned about three-quarters of all the land in England. This made them very rich.

The king gave land to his favourite nobles. In return, they had to be loyal to him and send soldiers for his army. Below them were the knights, who fought for and served the nobles.

This picture shows the coronation of King Edward I in 1274.

Working on the land

Most ordinary people were peasants. They spent part of each week working for their lord. In return, they were allowed to farm a small piece of land. Their lives were very hard. It was often a struggle to grow enough food to feed themselves and their families.

King Richard II addresses the peasants as Wat Tyler lies defeated.

THE PEASANTS' REVOLT

In June 1381, a group of peasants left their homes in Kent and marched to London. Their leader was Wat Tyler. The peasants were angry about their low wages and high taxes. Wat Tyler was killed, but King Richard II promised to help the peasants. However, once the **revolt** ended, the king went back on his promises.

Where would I live?

If you had been a peasant child in medieval Britain, you probably would have lived in a **cruck** house. These houses had wooden frames. The walls were made from wattle and daub – woven twigs covered with a sticky mixture of mud and straw. The roof was made from **thatch**. Windows were simply small holes in the walls with no glass.

Inside, your house had one room where your whole family lived, ate, and slept. The floor was bare earth, covered with straw. A fire kept the house warm, but also filled it with smoke because there was no chimney. There was very little furniture, and you often had to share your house with your family's animals.

Some medieval houses are still used as homes.

Conwy Castle in Wales was built for Edward I.

Rich people's homes

For a child of a lord or a knight, life was very different. You might live in a medieval **manor** house or castle, built from stone. You had private family rooms and wooden beds to sleep in, with mattresses stuffed with straw.

TOILETS

Peasant houses did not have bathrooms for washing or going to the toilet. The toilet was a bucket that was emptied every day into the nearest river or stream.

What would my childhood be like?

Medieval girls helped to spin wool.

From an early age, peasant children were expected to help their parents in the house and fields. You did simple jobs, such as fetching water or herding geese. Most peasant children did not go to school and could not read or write. When you were not working, you climbed trees, played ball games, made bows and arrows, or played with homemade dolls. You also spent a lot of your time at church.

In wealthy families, children usually started their education around the age of seven. If you were a girl, you learnt how to spin and sew, and how to run a home. Some boys went to school, where they learnt reading, writing, and some arithmetic (maths). If your father was a nobleman, you might be sent to a **monastery** to study with the **monks**, or you were sent away to be tutored in another nobleman's house.

MARRIAGE

In a noble family, parents arranged their children's marriages. Some couples only met for the first time just before their wedding day. Girls often got married very young – around the age of 12.

Here boys from wealthy families are doing lessons with their tutor.

What clothes would I wear?

If you were a peasant, you wore clothes made from rough wool or **linen**. You had underclothes made from linen to stop the wool making your skin itch. Boys wore tunics and hose (leggings). Girls wore long dresses. In cold weather, you wore a sheepskin cloak for warmth. Most poor people only had one set of clothes.

Many people wore shoes or boots made from leather.

In medieval times, most clothes were homemade. Women spun wool into thread. The thread was then woven into cloth. Making clothes took a long time and a lot of work. Peasants did not usually dye their wool, so their clothes were mostly brown, red, or grey.

LAWS FOR CLOTHES

Special laws were passed to stop ordinary people dressing in the same way as nobles. For example, only wives and daughters of wealthy men could wear velvet. Only noblemen were allowed to wear the latest fashion in pointed shoes.

Children from noble families had clothes made from finer fabrics, such silk, fine wool, and velvet. Clothes were brightly coloured and sometimes decorated with gold thread or fur.

This picture shows a knight and his lady, dressed in fine clothes. The richer you were, the finer and fancier your clothes became.

What would I eat and drink?

As a peasant child, your diet was mainly made up of bread and **pottage** (thick soup). Children from wealthier families ate many different foods – meat, fish, and rich puddings.

Peasant families ate what they could produce for themselves. They made dark, heavy bread from barley and rye. They made pottage from oats and vegetables, such as onions, cabbage, and leeks. Sometimes they ate meat, usually pork from their pigs. They cooked food on a stone hearth, or in an iron pot hung over the fire.

These peasants are throwing sticks at the trees, so acorns fall for the pigs to eat.

If you came from a noble family, your house had kitchens where cooks prepared your meals. You ate white bread made from wheat, and meat such as lamb, beef, deer, and rabbit. Rich households could also afford expensive spices, such as pepper, ginger, or nutmeg. These spices came from far away countries such as India and South East Asia. They were used for making sauces.

DRINKING ALE
Everyone, including children, drank ale. Water from rivers and streams was often too dirty to drink. Ale made from barley was the usual drink for breakfast, lunch, and supper.

What would I believe?

In medieval times, the Roman Catholic Church was very important in people's lives. The country was divided into **parishes,** each one with a priest. **Bishops** were in charge of a group of parishes called a **diocese**. At the head of the Church was the **Pope**.

Canterbury Cathedral in Kent was built in the 11th century and later rebuilt several times.

THE CANTERBURY TALES

Pilgrimages were popular in medieval times. In the late 1300s, a poet called Geoffrey Chaucer wrote *The Canterbury Tales*. These tell the story of **pilgrims** on their way to the shrine (holy place) at Canterbury. In 1170, Thomas Becket, the Archbishop of Canterbury, was murdered inside Canterbury Cathedral by four knights working for King Henry II.

This is the ruins of Rievaulx Abbey in Yorkshire. It was founded in 1132 by a group of monks.

One of the first events in your life was baptism. This was often done on the day you were born. You were taken to church, where the priest blessed you and bathed you with holy water. This ceremony welcomed you into the Church.

Monks and nuns

Some men and women left everyday life to go and live in **monasteries** or **convents**. They became **monks** or **nuns**. They spent their lives praying and helping others. Some were scholars who studied the Bible and other holy books, and wrote **manuscripts**.

What would I do when I grew up?

In a peasant family, you were likely to follow in your parents' footsteps and become a farmer. But you might have become a servant in a castle or **manor** house. Servants did all sorts of jobs, including washing, cooking, and cleaning.

Guilds

There were many different crafts and trades in medieval times. Almost all had their own **guilds**. The main aim of the guilds was to make sure that their members got a fair price for their work. Guilds also looked after their members if they were ill and could not work.

This guildhall in Lavenham, Suffolk was the centre of the town's cloth industry.

Many boys and some girls became **apprentices** and learnt a trade, such as carpentry or blacksmithing. Apprentices lived with their masters (teachers). It took many years for apprentices to learn all they needed to know and become masters in their own right.

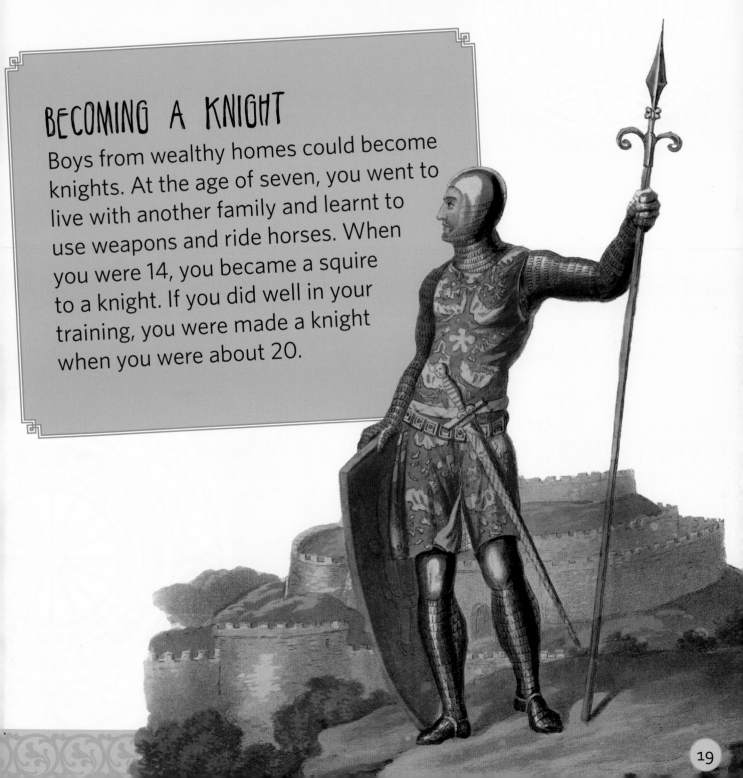

BECOMING A KNIGHT

Boys from wealthy homes could become knights. At the age of seven, you went to live with another family and learnt to use weapons and ride horses. When you were 14, you became a squire to a knight. If you did well in your training, you were made a knight when you were about 20.

How would I have fun?

Both children and adults looked forward to holy days, or holidays. At these times, such as Christmas or Easter, people stopped work to go to church, and to have fun at fairs.

Medieval fairs were exciting open-air markets. Merchants set out their goods on stalls. At the big fairs, there were all kinds of things for sale, such as spices or rugs. They were too expensive for most ordinary people to buy. If people got hungry, there were stalls selling snacks and small pies, called chewets.

This picture is of a crowded medieval fair.

There was lots of entertainment at fairs. People flocked to watch the acrobats, jugglers, stilt-walkers, and musicians. Dancing bears were also very popular.

This modern performance of a mystery play in York is telling the story of Noah's Ark.

Travelling players

In some cities, members of **guilds** put on "mystery plays". These plays told stories from the Bible. The players performed out on the streets. Their "stage" was a wagon that could be moved from place to place.

CHILDREN'S TOYS

Medieval children played with balls, dolls, sticks, marbles, and rattles. Balls were made from wood or leather. A popular game was nine-pin bowling. Girls' dolls were known as poppets and were usually made from cloth or wood.

What would happen if I was ill?

Towns and cities were filthy places in medieval times. Rubbish and dung (animal droppings) covered the streets. Water for drinking and washing was often dirty. Children got stomach upsets or more serious diseases from the dirty conditions.

THE PLAGUE

Between 1347 and 1350, a disease called the plague spread across Europe. It turned people's skin black and killed them in days. It became known as the Black Death. There was no cure for the plague in medieval times. So many people died that they were buried in big pits, with the bodies piled on top of each other.

Sick people visiting a medieval doctor – they did not always go home with a cure!

Doctors and wise women

If your family were wealthy, you could afford to see a doctor if you were ill. Medieval doctors looked at the colour of your skin and wee to try to work out what was wrong with you. A popular treatment was bloodletting. The doctor made a cut in your skin to allow your blood to flow out.

Most people were cared for at home. Girls often learnt from their mothers about the different plants and herbs used to make simple medicines. Sometimes, villages had a local "wise woman" – a healer who knew all about traditional cures.

After medieval Britain

At the Battle of Agincourt in 1415, the English, under Henry V, defeated the French.

The Hundred Years' War was a series of battles between England and France that lasted from 1337 to 1453. Ever since William the Conqueror came from Normandy to conquer England in 1066, the English kings had ruled parts of France. Edward III believed he should be king of all France, and set off with his army. This sparked more than 100 years of fighting.

It was also a time of war between England and Scotland. In 1296, Edward I invaded Scotland and took the Stone of Scone. This was the ancient stone used in ceremonies to crown Scottish kings and queens. But at the Battle of Bannockburn in 1314, the Scots defeated the English. In 1328, Edward III was forced to let Scotland become a free country.

York versus Lancaster

Medieval times ended with the Wars of the Roses (1455–1485) between two royal houses of England. The red rose was the symbol of the house of Lancaster. The white rose was the symbol of the house of York. In 1485, Lancastrian Henry Tudor finally defeated Richard III of York at the Battle of Bosworth, and seized the throne. This marked the start of the Tudor period.

Richard III of York's body was finally found in 2012, more than 500 years after his death.

How do we know?

There are many medieval castles all over Britain that give us a good idea of what medieval life was like. Castles were the homes of lords and knights, their families and servants. They were built of stone, often on hilltops to get a good view of the countryside in case of attack. When the lord was not away fighting for the king, he often held a great feast for his family, knights, and friends. The guests dressed in their best clothes and ate the finest food.

Three-handed drinking cups, like the one pictured, were used during medieval feasts, so the wine or beer could easily be shared.

This medieval brooch is mainly made of copper. It was found near Dover. The pin across the middle is shaped like a dagger. Guests wore brooches like this to feasts.

Timelines

Kings of England

1066–1087	William I the Conqueror
1087–1100	William II
1100–1135	Henry I
1135–1154	Stephen
1154–1189	Henry II
1189–1199	Richard I
1199–1216	John
1216–1272	Henry III
1272–1307	Edward I
1307–1327	Edward II
1327–1377	Edward III
1377–1399	Richard II
1399–1413	Henry IV
1413–1422	Henry V
1422–1461	Henry VI
1461–1483	Edward IV
1483	Edward V
1483–1485	Richard III

Kings and queens of Scotland

1016–1034	Malcolm II
1034–1040	Duncan I
1040–1057	Macbeth
1057–1058	Lulach
1058–1093	Malcolm III
1093–1097	Donald III
1094	Duncan II
1097–1107	Edgar
1107–1124	Alexander I
1124–1153	David I
1153–1165	Malcolm IV
1165–1214	William I
1216–1249	Alexander II
1249–1286	Alexander III
1286–1290	Margaret
1292–1296	John Balliol
1306–1329	Robert I the Bruce
1329–1371	David II
1371–1390	Robert II
1390–1406	Robert III
1406–1437	James I
1437–1460	James II
1460–1488	James III

Quiz

What do you know about life in medieval times? Try this quiz to find out!

1. What was a chewet?
   a medieval chewing gum
   b a delicious small pie
   c a small dog

2. In medieval times, who drank ale?
   a only the men
   b only the grown-ups
   c everyone!

3. What might a doctor suggest if you were ill?
   a making a cut to let the blood out
   b drinking medicines made from herbs
   c visiting your nearest holy shrine

4. What did Edward I steal from Scotland?
   a the crown jewels
   b the Stone of Scone
   c the Loch Ness monster

5. What was a cruck house?
   a a house with a wooden frame
   b a hen house
   c a crooked house

5. a
4. b
3. trick question! a, b, and c
2. c
1. b
Answers

Glossary

abbot head of a monastery

apprentice person who is learning a trade

bishop senior member of the Christian church, in charge of a diocese

convent community of nuns

cruck curved piece of wood that supports a roof

diocese group of churches under the care of a bishop

guild organization made up of members that work in the same craft or trade

linen cloth made from the flax plant

manor in medieval times, a lord's land, including all the land he rents to other people to live on

manuscript document that is written by hand

monastery community of monks

monk man who lives in a monastery and dedicates his life to God

nun member of a women's religious community. Nuns live in a convent.

parish church district with its own church building and priest

pilgrim person who makes a journey to a holy place for religious reasons

Pope head of the Roman Catholic Church, based in Rome, Italy

pottage type of thick soup made from oats and vegetables

revolt rebellion

thatch roof made from straw

Find out more

Books

Medieval Life (Eyewitness Project Books), (Dorling Kindersley, 2009)

The Kingfisher Atlas of the Medieval World, Simon Adams (Kingfisher, 2007)

The Usborne Medieval World, Jane Bingham (Usborne, 2012)

Websites

www.bbc.co.uk/history/forkids/index.shtml
This website is packed with information about British and world history, with lots of facts and hands-on activities, including building your own castle.

www.bbc.co.uk/history/interactive/timelines/british/index_embed.shtml
Click on "Middle Ages" on this interactive timeline.

www.educationscotland.gov.uk/scotlandshistory/medievallife/index.asp
Find out more about medieval life in Scotland.

resources.woodlands-junior.kent.sch.uk/customs/questions/history. html#Medieval
Information about medieval Britain can be found on the Woodlands Junior site.

Places to visit

There are many medieval castles and manor houses to visit all over Britain. You can find out about them through the following organizations:

English Heritage
www.english-heritage.org.uk

The National Trust in England, Wales, and Northern Ireland
www.nationaltrust.org.uk

The National Trust of Scotland
www.nts.org.uk

Index